MW01698029

Roar into Spelling

a learning activity book

Color Edition

by
Marie Rippel
and
Samantha Johnson

All About® Spelling
Level 3

Printed in the United States of America

Color Edition
v. 1.0.0

All About® Learning Press, Inc.
615 Commerce Loop
Eagle River, WI 54521

ISBN 978-1-959954-00-2

Editor:	Renée LaTulippe
Cover Illustration:	Dave LaTulippe
Page Layout:	Shanna Behrens, Emily F. Johnson
Illustrator:	Donna Goeddaeus
Activity Colorization:	Shanna Behrens, Emily F. Johnson

The Level 3 *Roar into Spelling* activity book is part of the *All About® Spelling* program.

For more books in this series, go to www.AllAboutSpelling.com.

Hello!

Welcome to *Roar into Spelling*!

This activity book is a fun and essential part of Level 3 of the *All About Spelling* program. On the pages that follow, you'll find:

- Progress Chart
- Activity Sheets
- Spelling Rule Posters
- Word Banks
- Advanced Application Sheets
- Writing Station Sheets
- Certificate of Achievement

The lesson plans in the Teacher's Manual will tell you exactly which pages you'll need for each lesson and provide you with complete instructions on how to use each activity sheet. The pages are perforated for easy removal.

The activities in this book will help your student master spelling.

Enjoy your lessons!

Marie Rippel

All About® Spelling

Level 3 - Progress Chart

Name ______________________________

1 2 3 4 5 6 7 8 9 10 11 12 13 14 15 16 17 18 19 20 21 22 23 24 25 26 27 28 29 30

Rules for
Syllable Division

1 Compound Words Rule

Divide compound words into smaller words.

d u s t   m o p

2 Two Consonants Rule

Point to the vowels. If there are two consonants between them, we usually divide between the consonants.

n a p   k i n

3 One Consonant Rule

Part 1: Point to the vowels. If there is one consonant between them, we usually divide before the consonant.

b r o   k e n

Part 2: If that doesn't make a real word, move the consonant to the first syllable.

r o b   i n

p o ck   e t

Note: Keep consonant teams together.

4 Pickle Syllables Rule

When a word ends in a Pickle syllable, count back three letters from the end and divide.

s t a   p l e

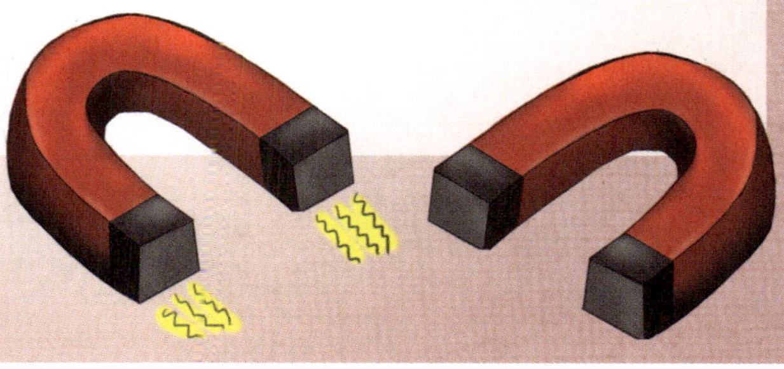

5 Suffixes Rule

Consonant suffixes form their own syllables, with the exception of suffix s.

g r a c e | ful

b ea k s

Vowel suffixes usually form their own syllables, although they often grab the preceding consonant.

s w i m | m er

w a | v ing

6 Prefixes Rule

Divide after a prefix.

pre | p l a n

7 Three Consonants Rule

Part 1: Point to the vowels. If there are three consonants between them, we usually divide after the first consonant.

ch i l | d r e n

Part 2: If that doesn't make a real word, divide after the second consonant.

p u m p | k i n

Note: Keep consonant teams together.

8 Two Vowels Rule

When two vowels are together, divide between them.

Note: Keep vowel teams together.

d i | e t

The Jobs of Silent E

1 Silent E can make the **vowel before it long**. Silent E does this job in 50% of words ending in e.

g a m e

2 Silent E can make **c and g soft**.

f e n c e   ch ar g e

3 Silent E keeps **u and v** from being the **last letter in a word**.

c l u e   g i v e

4 Silent E shows that the word **is not plural**.

r i n s   r i n s e

5 Silent E **adds a vowel to a Pickle syllable**. Every syllable needs a vowel.

a p   p l e

6 Silent E makes **th say its second sound**, /th/.

t ee th e   b a th e

7 Silent E **clarifies the meaning** of the word.

b y   b y e

aw   aw e

What is Elwood's favorite food?

What is Elwood's favorite season?

What is Elwood's favorite color?

What is Elwood's favorite place?

What is Elwood's favorite way to travel?

What is Elwood's favorite thing to wear?

AI
AY

pl___

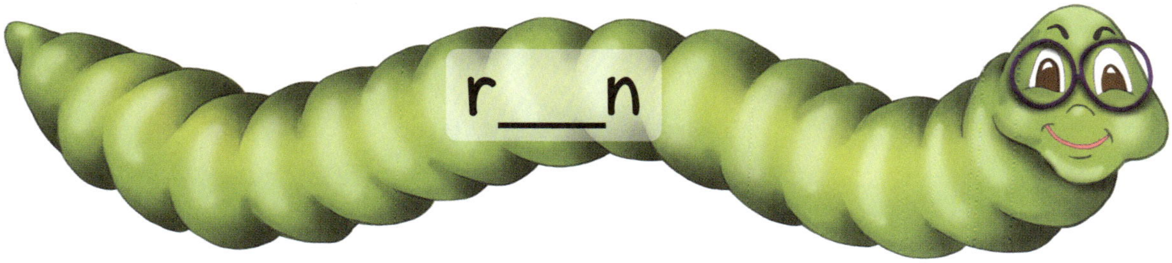
r___n

tod___

f___l

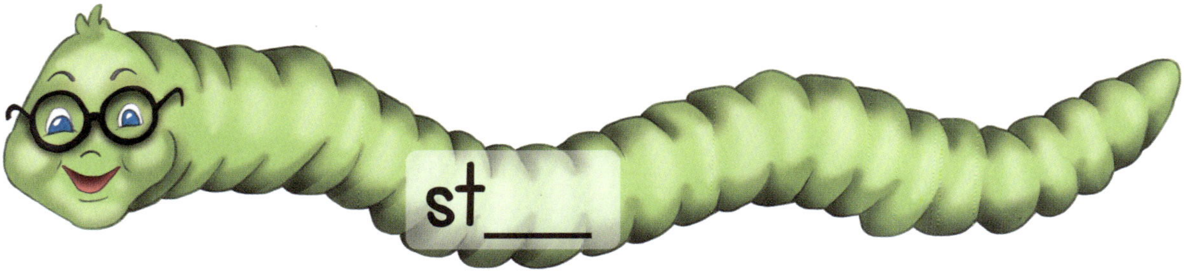
st___

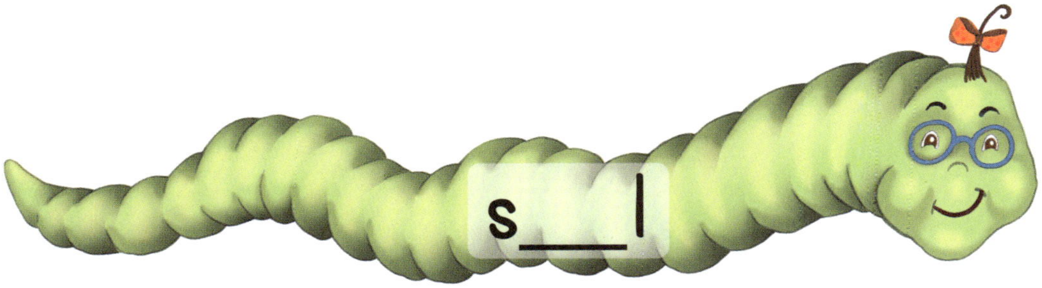
s___l

tr___

w___t

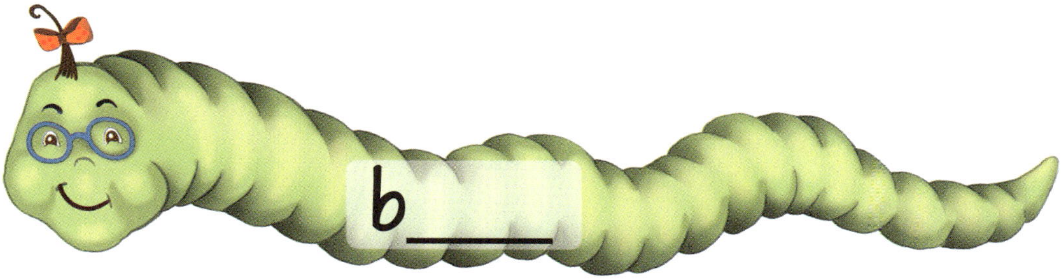
b___

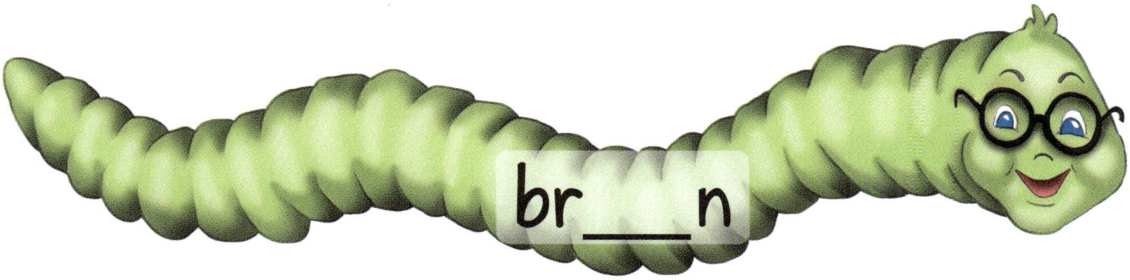
br___n

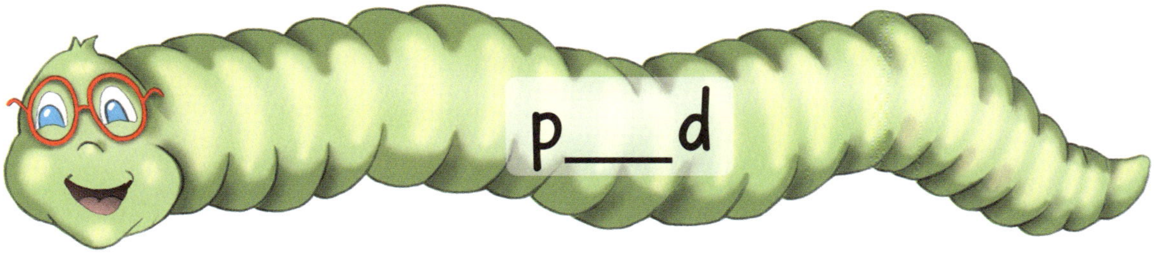
p___d

spr___

50
Fun Ideas for

James
Gets
the

:
28 Great Facts

Kelly's New

The Guide
to

How to Buy

99 Games
to
Play with

the Easy Way

:
The Best
Methods

Word Bank for AY and AI

AY

ray	clay	stay	way	maybe
tray	spray	bay	play	today
pay	day	gray	lay	say
okay	May	stray	pray	hay

AI

paid	faith	air	hail	paint
quail	claim	nail	stairs	pail
pair	frail	tail	bail	wait
mailbox	waist	chair	trail	rain
brain	fail	pain	bait	sail
snail	rail	saint	aim	fair
jail	drain	faint	grain	mail
plain	chain	main	stain	train

Advanced Application

1. hoo ____________
2. ____________ bow
3. side ____________
4. ____________ grounds
5. ____________ land
6. por ____________
7. para ____________ ing
8. ____________ ness
9. do ____________
10. ____________ ment
11. ____________ orbird
12. dis ____________

Word Sort for Long A

a	a-e	ay	ai
acorn	maze	day	mail

cable	crazy		
taper	table	agent	acorn
baby	basic	apron	flaky
maple	bacon	staple	brave
cake	place	made	grain
paid	bail	hay	okay

Homophones Book

This book belongs to

(Your name here)

All About® Spelling

sun one

here by

won son

buy hear

scent?

cent?

dear?
deer?

hare?
hair?

Silent E Book

This book belongs to

____
(Your name here)

All About® Spelling

13 __________ 19 __________

14 __________ 20 __________

15 __________ 21 __________

16 __________ 22 __________

17 __________ 23 __________

18 __________ 24 __________

Rule Breakers Ending in Silent E

Silent E is sometimes added for historical purposes. For example, centuries ago the final e was actually pronounced in words such as *some* and *none*. And sometimes we don't know why Silent E was added. We treat these words as Rule Breakers.

1. gone ________
2. ________
3. ________
4. ________
5. ________
6. ________
7. ________
8. ________
9. ________
10. ________
11. ________
12. ________

Summary of Jobs of Silent E

Job 1: Silent E can make the vowel before it long.

Job 2: Silent E can make c and g soft.

Job 3: Silent E keeps u and v from being the last letter in a word.

Job 4: Silent E shows that the word is not plural.

Job 5: Silent E adds a vowel to a Pickle syllable.

Job 6: Silent E makes th say its second sound, /t̶h̶/.

Job 7: Silent E clarifies the meaning of the word.

Job #1

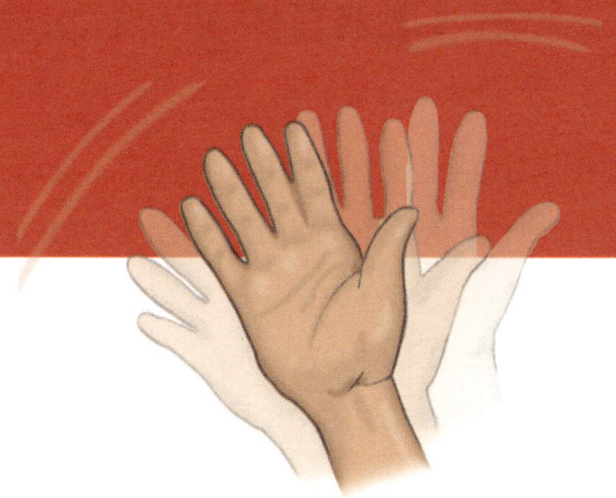

Silent E can make the vowel before it long.

1. dime
2. ______
3. ______
4. ______
5. ______
6. ______
7. ______
8. ______
9. ______
10. ______
11. ______
12. ______
13. ______
14. ______
15. ______
16. ______
17. ______
18. ______
19. ______
20. ______
21. ______
22. ______
23. ______
24. ______

Job #7

Silent E clarifies the meaning of a word.

1. bye
2.
3.
4.
5.
6.
7.
8.
9.
10.
11.
12.
13.
14.
15.
16.
17.
18.
19.
20.
21.
22.
23.
24.

Job #2

Silent E can make c and g soft.

1. orange ______
2. ______
3. ______
4. ______
5. ______
6. ______
7. ______
8. ______
9. ______
10. ______
11. ______
12. ______
13. ______
14. ______
15. ______
16. ______
17. ______
18. ______
19. ______
20. ______
21. ______
22. ______
23. ______
24. ______

Job #6

Silent E makes th say its second sound, /th/.

1 bathe ______ 7 ______ 13 ______ 19 ______

2 ______ 8 ______ 14 ______ 20 ______

3 ______ 9 ______ 15 ______ 21 ______

4 ______ 10 ______ 16 ______ 22 ______

5 ______ 11 ______ 17 ______ 23 ______

6 ______ 12 ______ 18 ______ 24 ______

Job #3

Silent E keeps u and v from being the last letter in a word.

1. glue ______
2. ______
3. ______
4. ______
5. ______
6. ______
7. ______
8. ______
9. ______
10. ______
11. ______
12. ______
13. ______
14. ______
15. ______
16. ______
17. ______
18. ______
19. ______
20. ______
21. ______
22. ______
23. ______
24. ______

Job #5

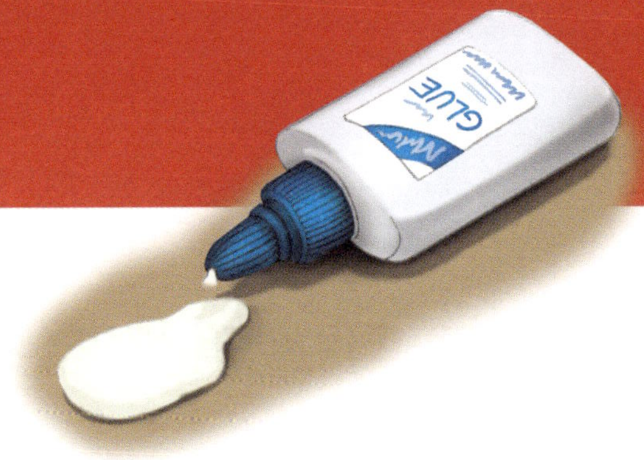

Silent E adds a vowel to a Pickle syllable.

1 candle

2 ______

3 ______

4 ______

5 ______

6 ______

7 ______

8 ______

9 ______

10 ______

11 ______

12 ______

13 ______

14 ______

15 ______

16 ______

17 ______

18 ______

19 ______

20 ______

21 ______

22 ______

23 ______

24 ______

Job #4

Silent E shows that the word is not plural.

1. house
2. ______
3. ______
4. ______
5. ______
6. ______
7. ______
8. ______
9. ______
10. ______
11. ______
12. ______
13. ______
14. ______
15. ______
16. ______
17. ______
18. ______
19. ______
20. ______
21. ______
22. ______
23. ______
24. ______

PICKLES

able	title	maple
uncle	gentle	handle
silent	outside	fifteen
became	enjoy	chime

Don't put the pickles next to the ______________.

Keep the pickles out of the ______________!

I checked the ______________ but the pickles weren't there!

I can't wait to tell the pickles about the ______________.

The ______________ is a great place to eat pickles!

I dropped sixteen pickles by the ______________.

My dog ate a ______________, but he won't eat pickles.

Fred took a photo of the pickles inside the ______________.

________	________	________	________
________	________	________	________

Word Bank for Pickle Syllables (Part 1)

gentle	able	simple	uncle	stable
bundle	maple	cradle	mumble	title
Bible	tremble	bumble	idle	gable
grumble	staple	table	cable	handle
tumble	noble	fable	candle	

Rule Breaker

said	gone

Advanced Application

1. ______ man
2. ______ spoon
3. ______ light
4. ______ s
5. un ______
6. ______ ness
7. grand ______
8. ______ weed
9. ______ bars
10. ______ woman
11. ______ mate
12. ______ song

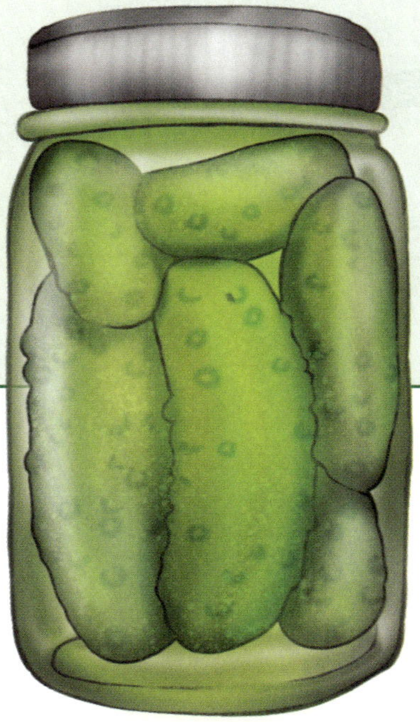

Open
Closed

little	table	puddle
uncle	middle	maple
able	apple	candle
gentle	staple	bubble
giggle	puzzle	handle

Word Bank for Pickle Syllables (Part 2)

kettle	drizzle	giggle	waffle	sizzle
wiggle	stubble	tattle	paddle	apple

topple	jiggle	riddle	scuffle	juggle
goggles	ripple	saddle	little	shuttle

nibble	cuddle	middle	puzzle	bottle
dribble	pebble	battle	ruffle	dazzle
puddle				

bubble

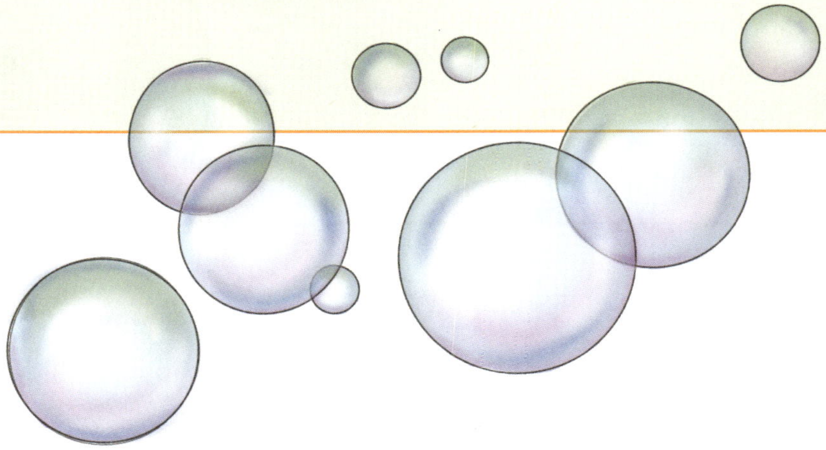

Advanced Application

1. tea ______
2. be ______
3. ______ gum
4. ______ bags
5. pine ______
6. ______ s
7. ______ brush
8. ______ man
9. ______ drum
10. ______ board
11. ______ ments
12. ______ stompers

Advanced Application

1. wel__________
2. dor__________
3. __________chase
4. out__________
5. __________theless
6. __________ware
7. __________s
8. __________point
9. __________s
10. quarrel__________
11. swash__________

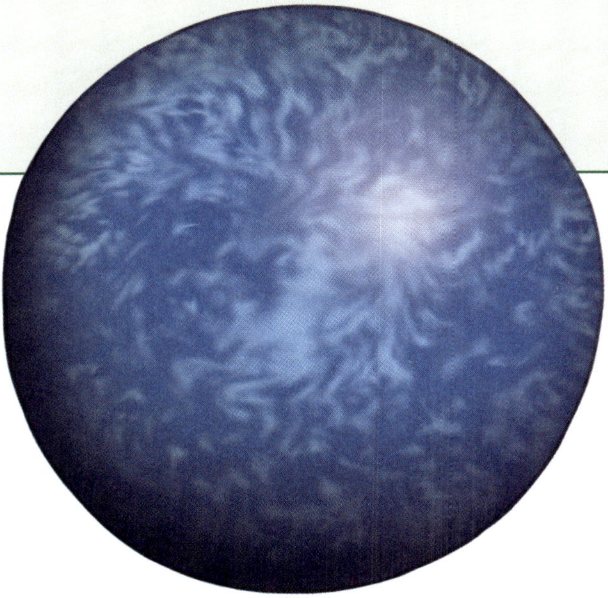

Word Bank for UR

spur	murmur	blur	turn	disturb
urge	churn	return	fur	surf
curb	lurk	slurp	blurt	hurt
burst	nurse	burn	urgent	purple
survive	purse	hurdle	curve	church
turtle	curl	gurgle		

yogurt

Advanced Application

1. noc ______________ al
2. out ______________
3. ______________ ry
4. ______________ icues
5. ______________ ed
6. ______________ ers
7. au ______________
8. ______________ ed
9. ______________ able
10. ______________ ing
11. ______________ ed
12. ______________ s

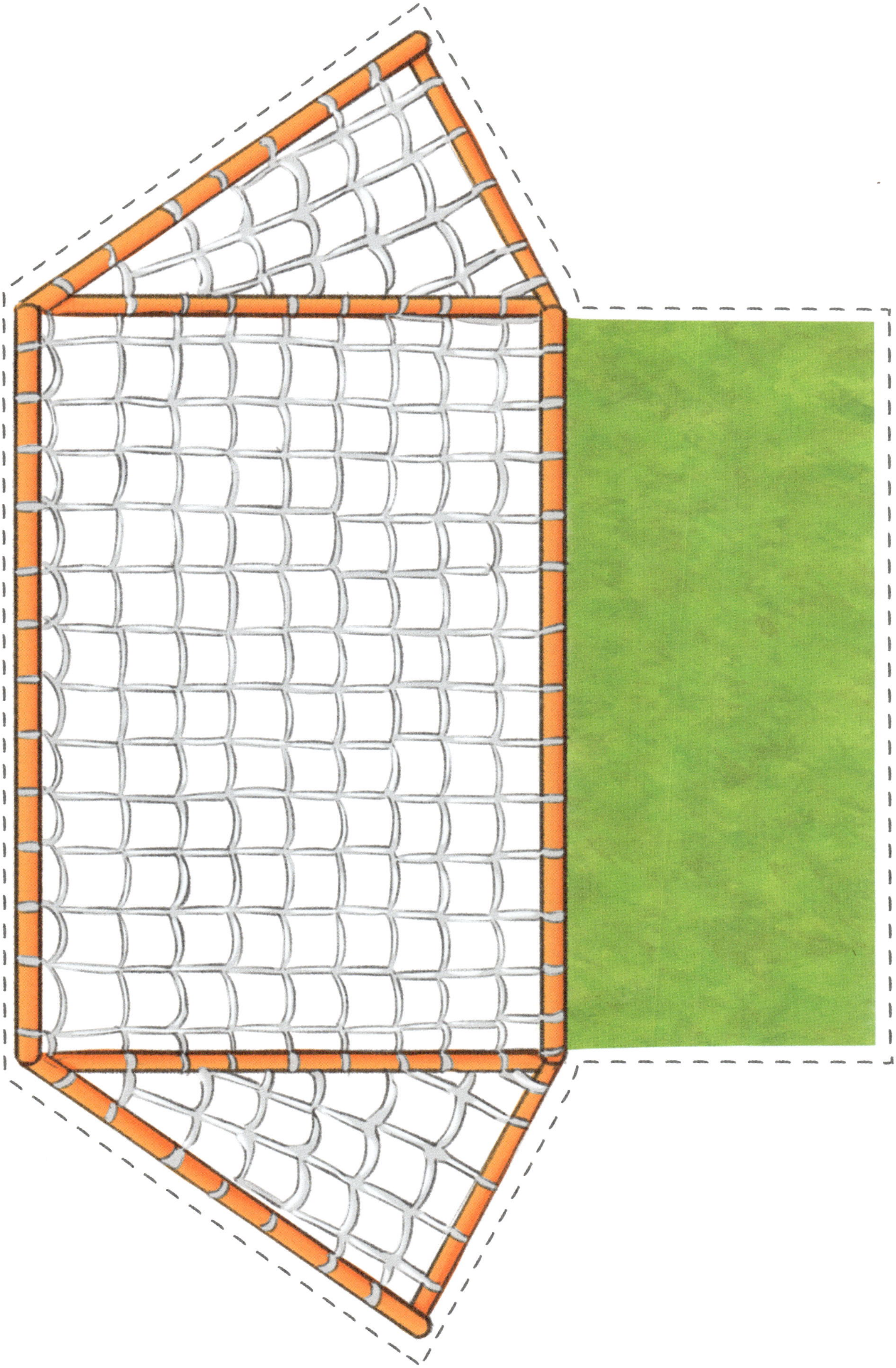

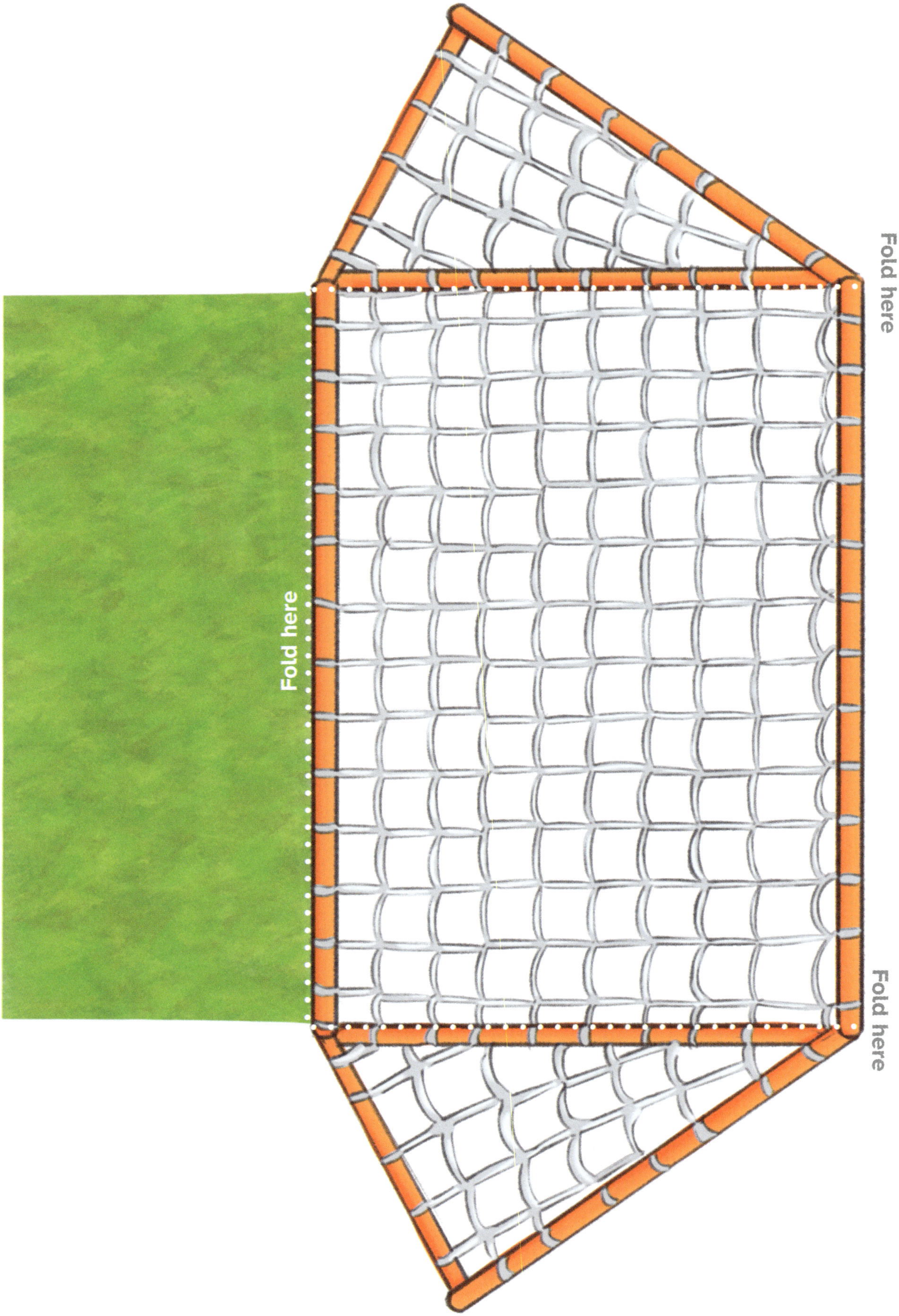
Fold here
Fold here
Fold here

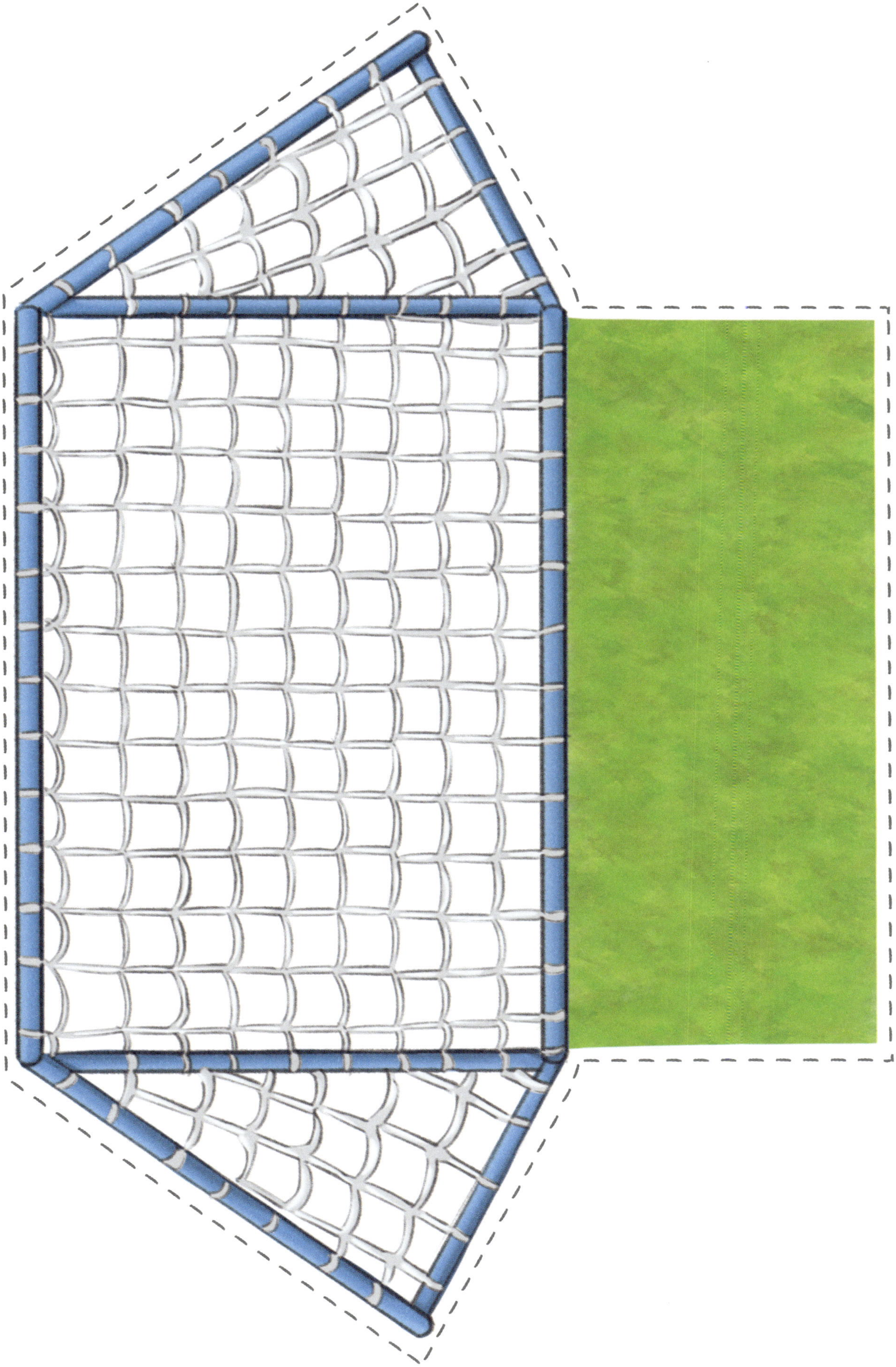

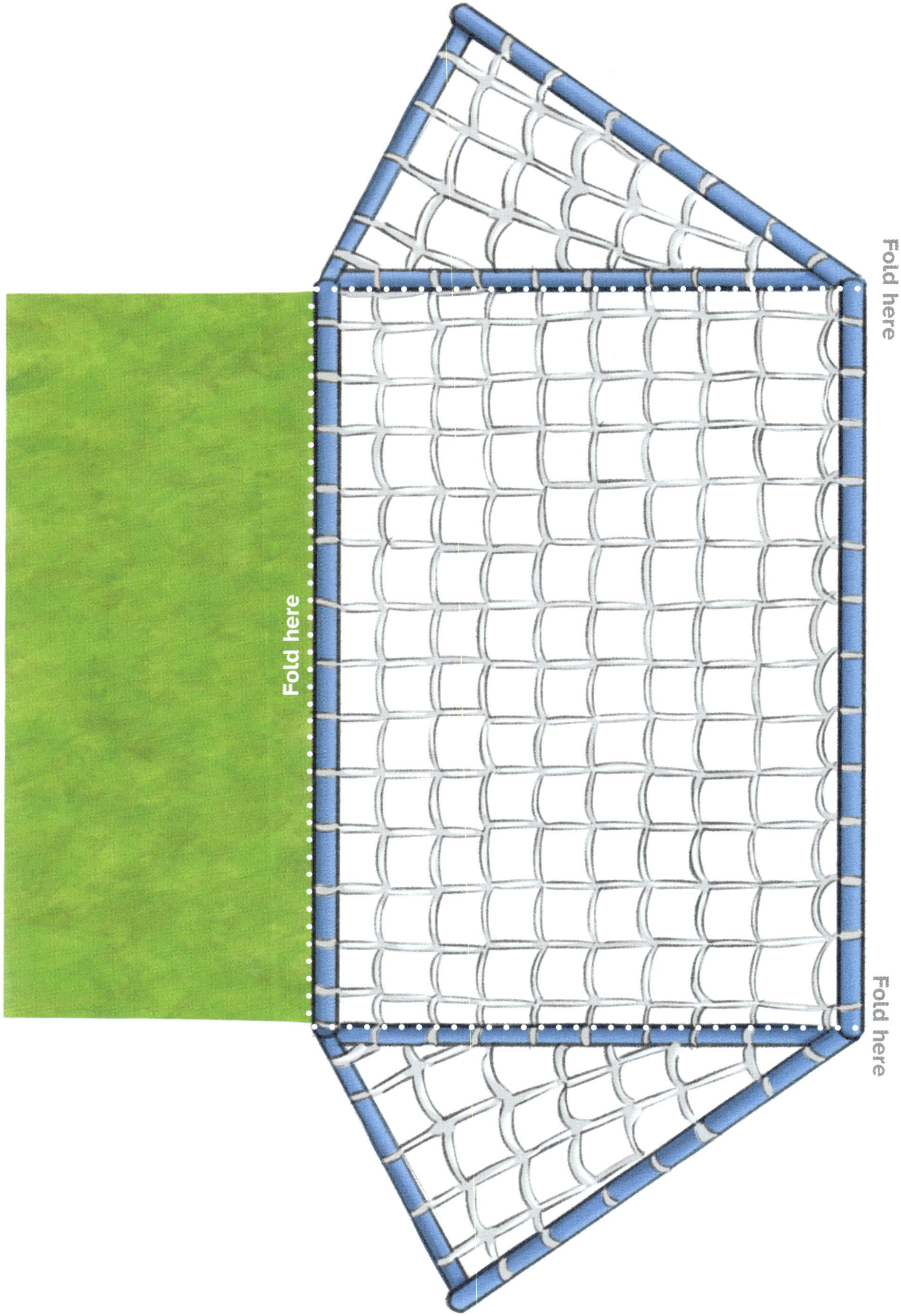
Fold here
Fold here
Fold here

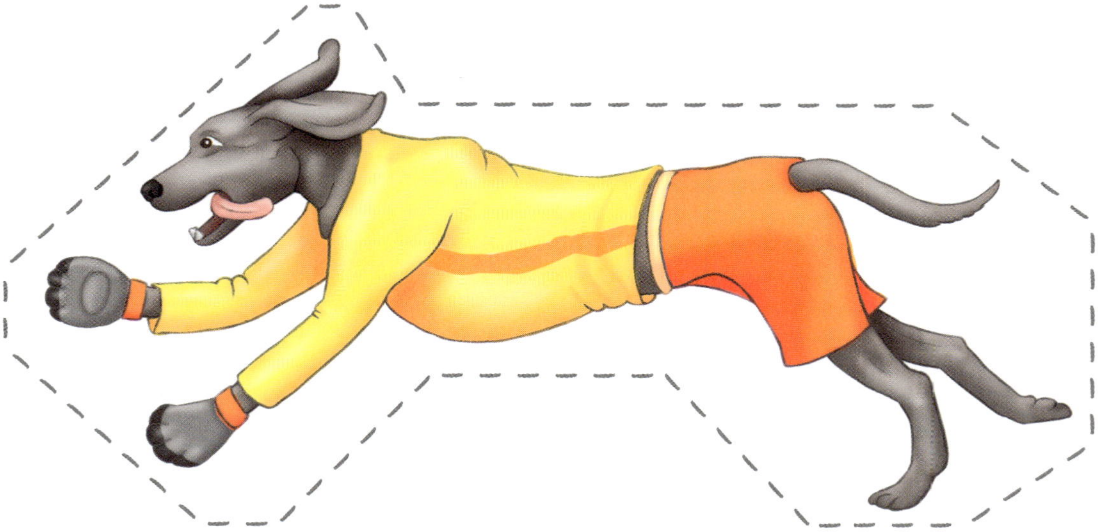

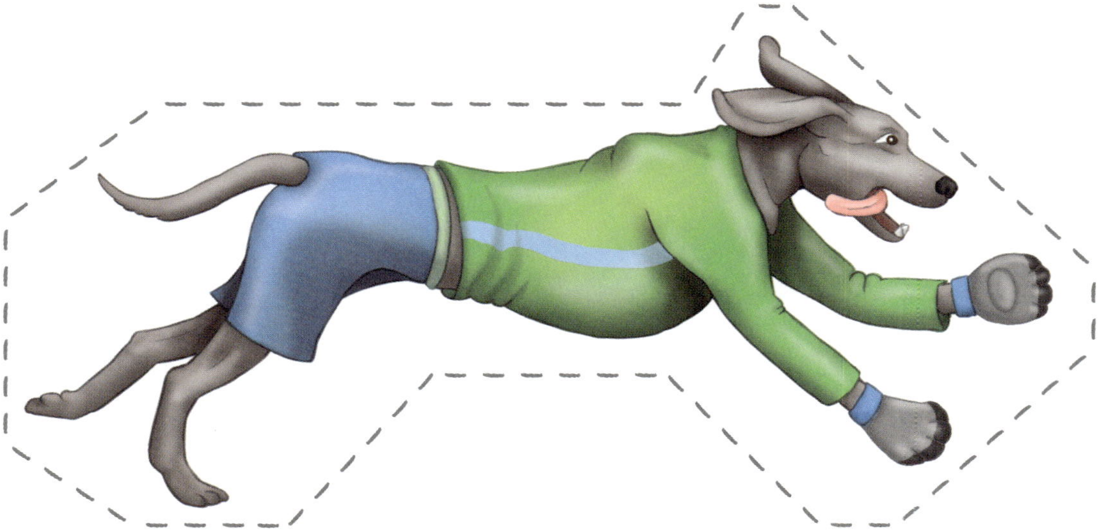

Tape pencil or marker here

Tape pencil or marker here

Advanced Application

1. ______ birds
2. ______ tail
3. ______ bones
4. ______ like
5. under ______
6. ______ sitter
7. ______ goers
8. inter ______
9. ______ abouts
10. ______ ing
11. ______ fore
12. un ______

The Double Consonant Rule

All About® Spelling
Level 3, Lesson 11

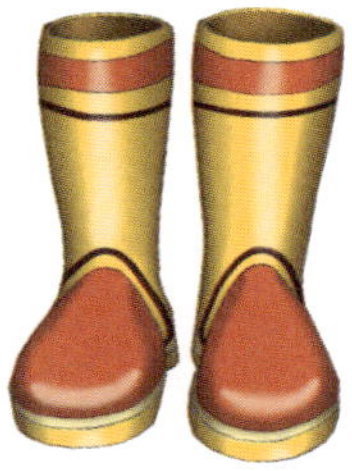

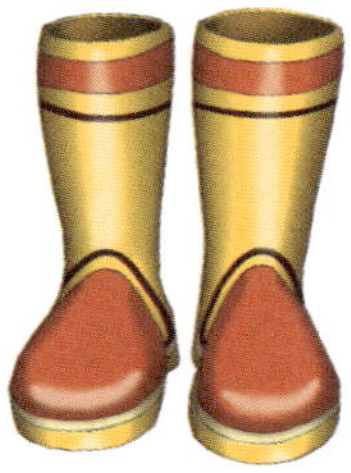

Word Bank for Double Consonants

Middle Consonant Is Doubled

penny	supper	Ellen	bonnet	mitten
silly	dinner	summit	sudden	jelly

sonnet	happy	rabbit	summer	comment
kitten	pollen	granny	puppet	happen

taffy	muffin	Dennis	hobby

Middle Consonant Is Not Doubled

city	body	ever	never	river
liver	copy	every		

Rule Breaker

are

Advanced Application

1. sun__________
2. __________ary
3. __________s
4. __________scape
5. jack__________
6. __________time
7. __________ing
8. __________ish
9. __________ly
10. __________guard
11. un__________
12. __________weight

OA
OW

goat	moan	soap
load	foal	oak
snow	blow	throw
glow	tow	crow

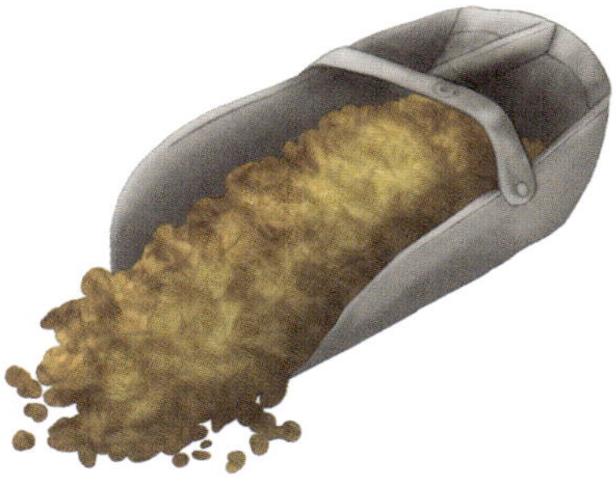

Word Bank for OA and OW

OA

float	cloak	soap	load	toast
coach	throat	oak	boat	soar
board	goat	road	foam	railroad
roar	coal	roast	soak	coat
oar	foal	coast	goal	loaf
toad	loan	moan	oats	groan

OW

follow	shadow	grow	row	mow
elbow	crow	flow	willow	own
show	pillow	blow	sow	yellow
glow	window	hollow	throw	low
grown	bow	slow	tow	snow

Advanced Application

1. ____________flakes
2. petti____________
3. ____________er
4. ____________ing
5. steam____________
6. ____________stopper
7. ____________stone
8. ____________less
9. ____________stool
10. ____________y
11. scare____________
12. ____________runner

Word Sort for Long O

o	o-e	oa	ow
hotel	rope	oak	blow

______	______	______	______
______	______	______	______
______	______	______	bolt
bonus	broken	robot	frozen
okay	moment	rodent	protect
omit	note	doze	cope
bone	pose	stone	soap
goat	yellow	shadow	hero

The **Consonant Suffix** Rule

kind + ness
kindness

help + ful
helpful

soft + ly
softly

When adding a consonant suffix, don't change the base word.

All About® Spelling
Level 3, Lesson 15

The 1-1-1 Rule

hot + est
hottest

fur + y
furry

sip + ing
sipping

If there is ...

- 1 syllable
- 1 vowel
- 1 consonant at the end

... double the consonant before adding a vowel suffix.

Do not double X, Y, or Z.

ALL ABOUT® Spelling
Level 3, Lesson 16

1 syllable
+
1 vowel
+
1 consonant
at the end
sky
sun
stop
dark
step
help
grass
fun
zip
play
hot
grab
big
nap
dirt
sleep

Double It!

Let's practice the 1+1+1 rule!

If there is ...

1 syllable + 1 vowel + 1 consonant at the end, double the consonant before adding a vowel suffix.

1. sit + ing = ____________
2. sun + y = ____________
3. nap + ing = ____________
4. run + er = ____________

5. mud + y = ____________
6. hop + ing = ____________
7. dig + er = ____________

Acacia Tree

Buffalo Thorn Fruit

Jackalberry Tree

Rhodes Grass

Baobab Tree

Lion's Eye

Mongongo

Candelabra Tree

Whistling Thorn

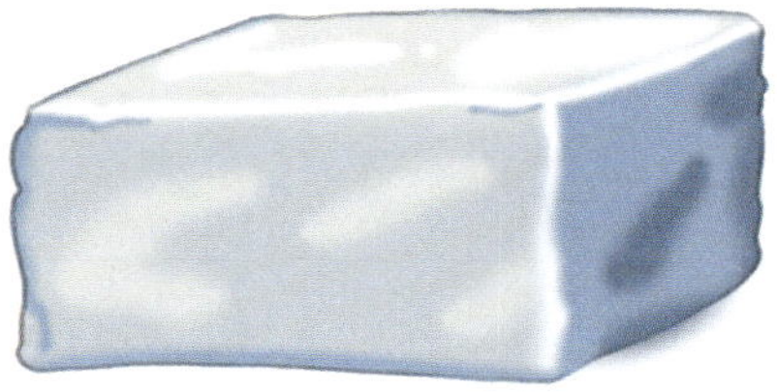
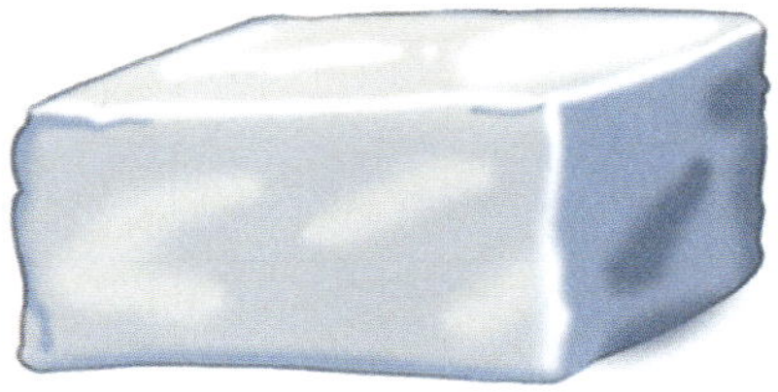
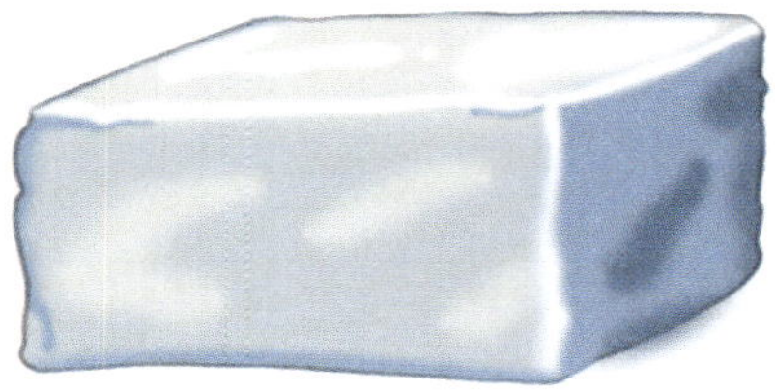
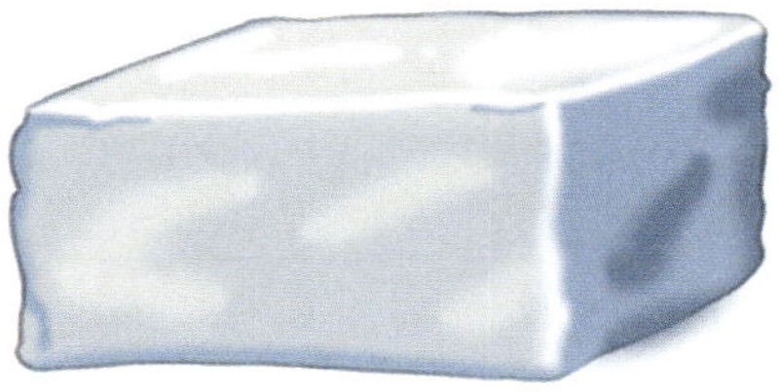
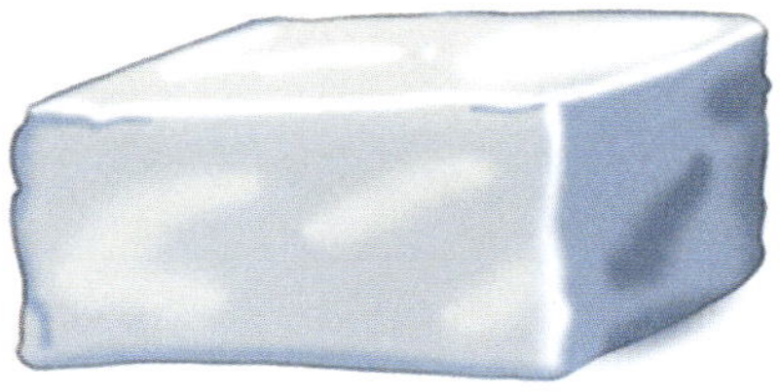
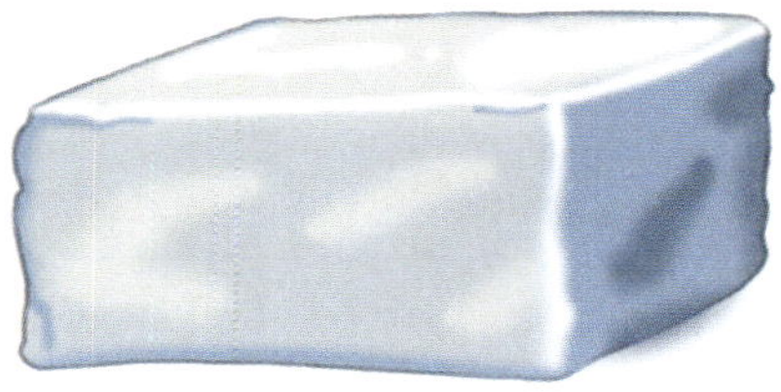
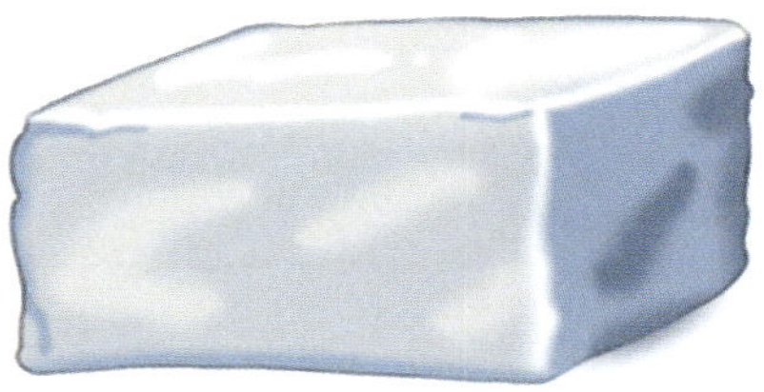
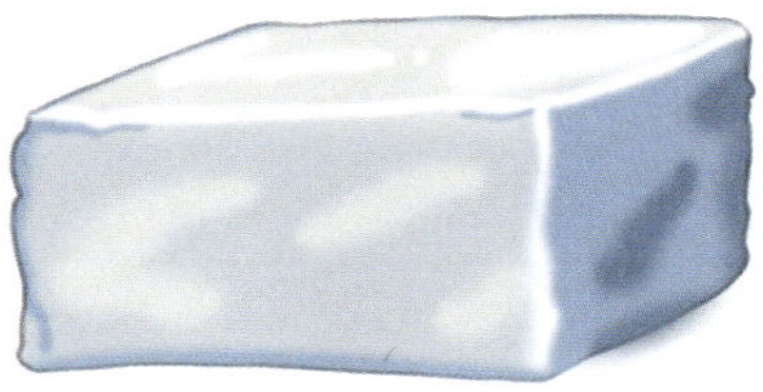
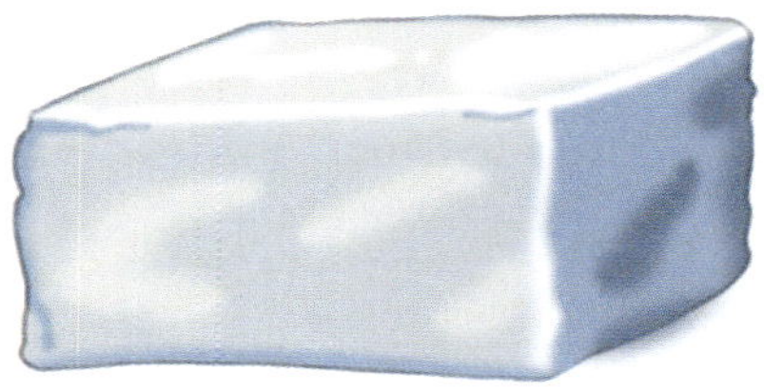

Word Bank for OO

goose	booth	soon	cool	loose
zoo	shampoo	toot	moon	gloomy
proof	food	smooth	boo	poof
drool	moo	loop	spoon	igloo
moose	bedroom	too	broom	droop
tooth	pooch	root	stool	rooster
snoop	noodle	spooky	cartoon	pool
roof	hoot	boot	bloom	noon
mood	toolbox	loom	fool	spool
doom	room	scooter	spoonful	tool
hoop				

Rule Breaker

any	many

Writing Station

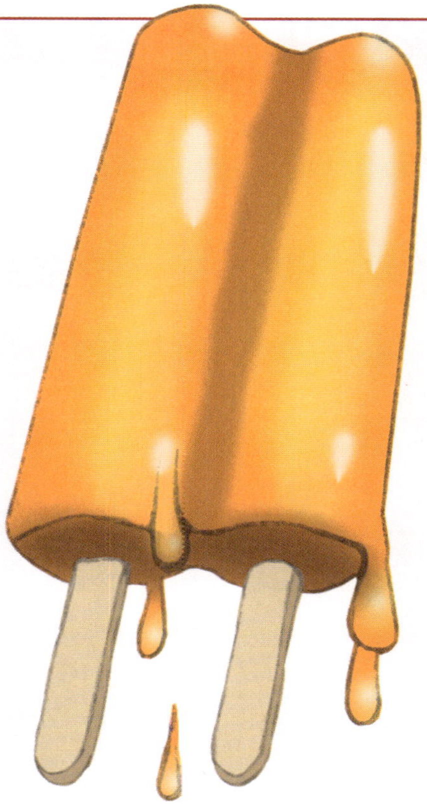

Words

1 ______________________

2 ______________________

3 ______________________

4 ______________________

5 ______________________

Sentences

1 ______________________

2 ______________________

3 ______________________

4 ______________________

5 ______________________

Advanced Application

1. ka ______________
2. ______________ ache
3. leg ______________
4. mon ______________
5. ______________ ie
6. ______________ flesh
7. ______________ less
8. ______________ ing
9. ______________ er
10. ______________ skirts
11. ______________ walk
12. tom ______________ ery

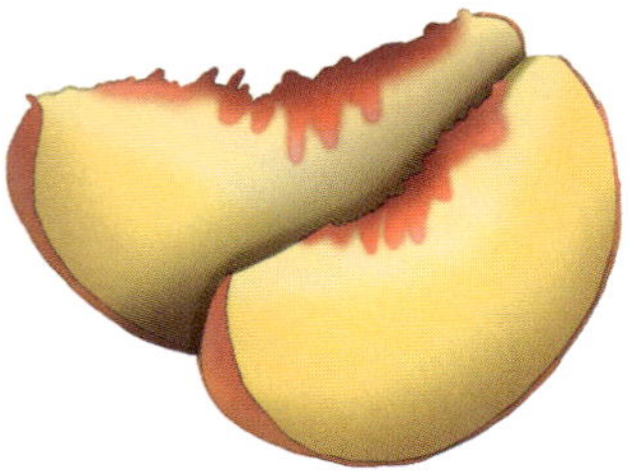
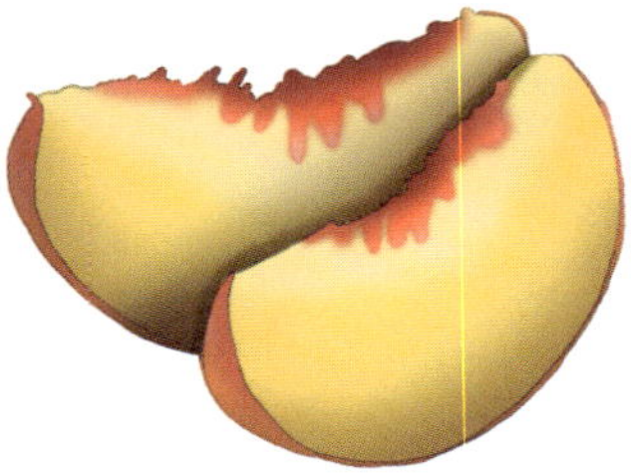
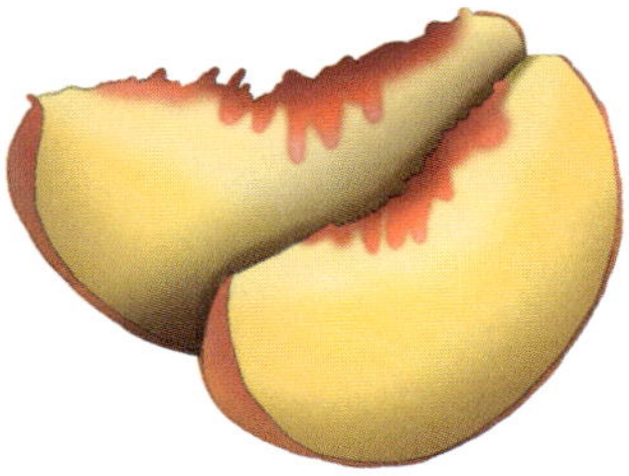

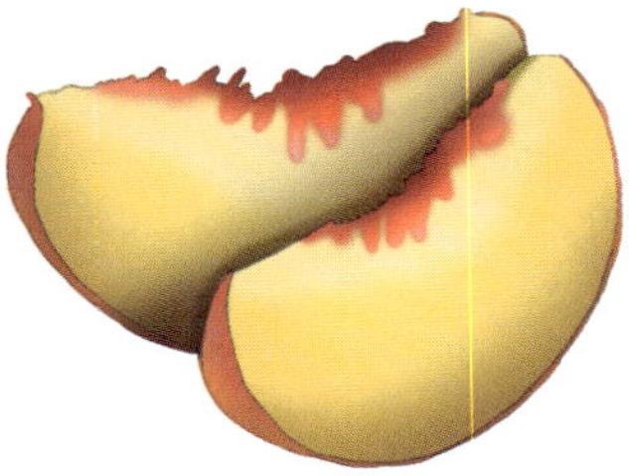
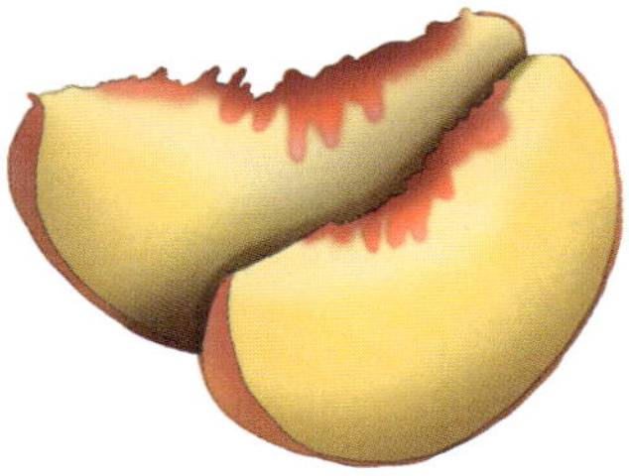
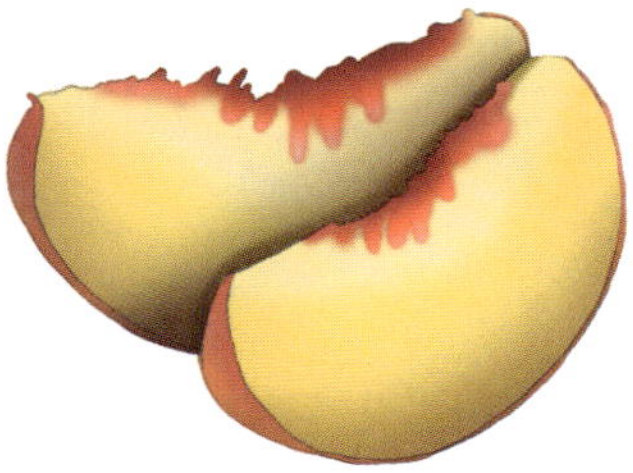
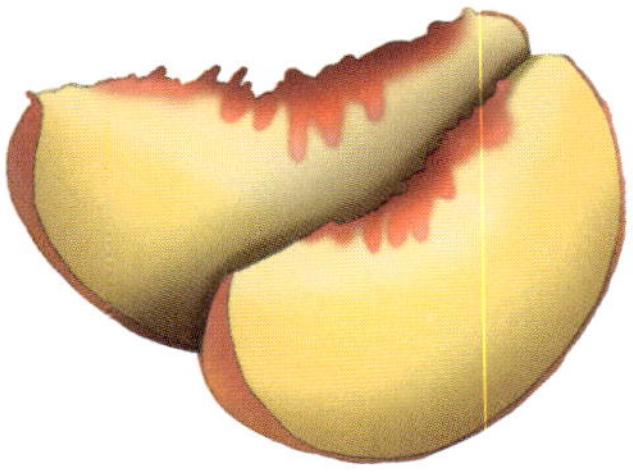
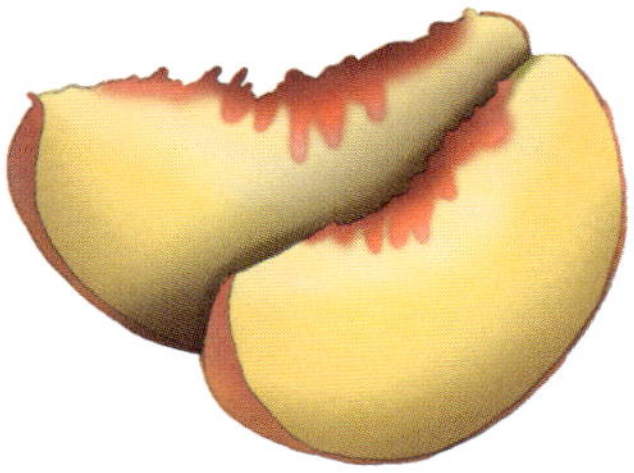
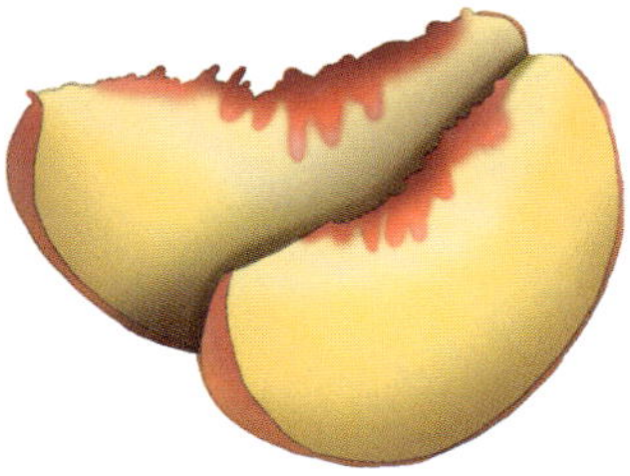
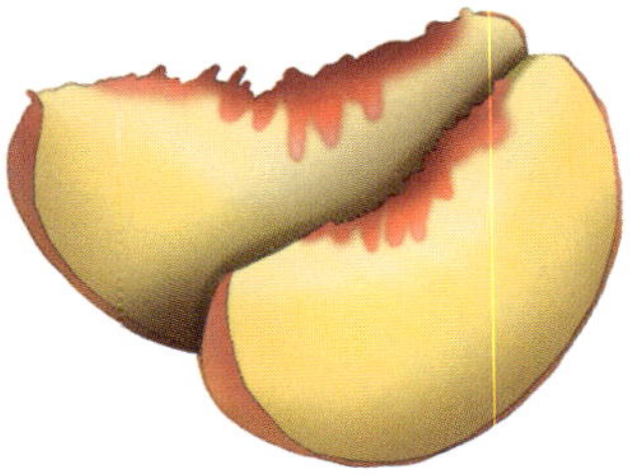
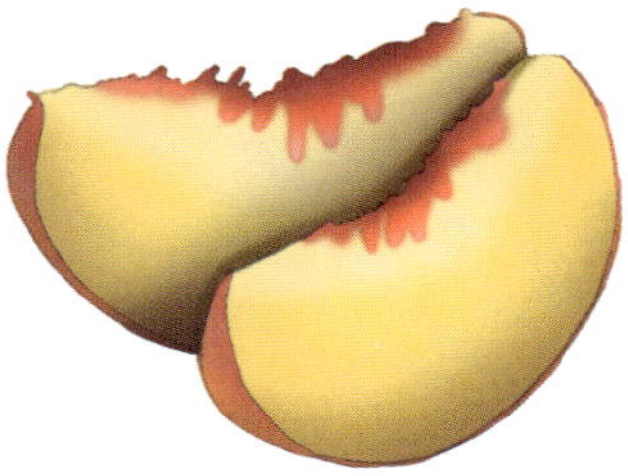

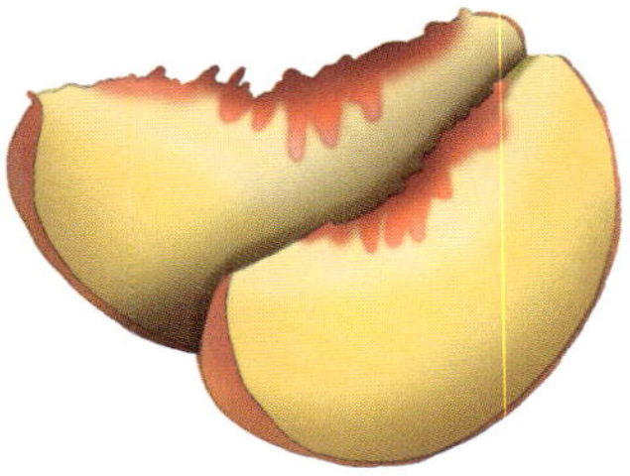
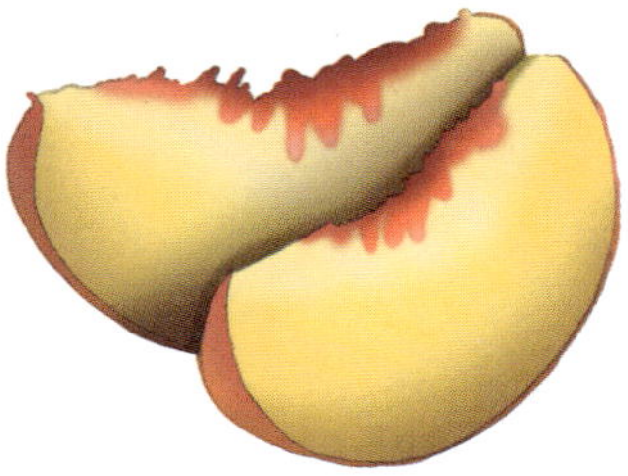

Word Bank for EA

peach	gear	bleach	tea	heal
cream	leak	eat	deal	clean
meal	steal	peace	sea	beaver
weak	dream	easy	tease	lead
eagle	pea	speak	bean	heat
near	real	peanut	seal	beach
mean	east	fear	ear	leash
scream	leave	clear	beak	year
meat	lean	breathe	beagle	wheat
leaf	dear	each	teach	neat
reach	please	read	hear	team

Writing Station

Words

1.
2.
3.
4.
5.

Sentences

1.
2.
3.
4.
5.

Advanced Application

1. ____________ going
2. day ____________ er
3. ____________ er
4. ____________ ingly
5. ____________ ling
6. ____________ ery
7. ____________ say
8. ____________ taster
9. ____________ proof
10. ____________ headed
11. ____________ bound
12. jelly ____________ s

Word Sort for Long E

e	e-e	ee	ea	y
be	theme	queen	seashell	bossy

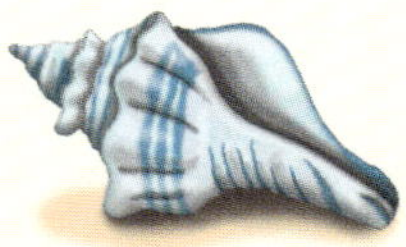

________	________	________	________
________	________	________	________
________	________	here	we
began	relax	demand	evil
zero	erase	ego	me
seed	deep	year	speak
fairy	twenty	study	ruby
dainty	zany	envy	county

Writing Station

Words

1

2

3

4

5

Sentences

1

2

3

4

5

The Past Tense Rule

landed
played
clapped

All About® Spelling

Level 3, Lesson 21

Word Sort for ED

/ĕd/	/d/	/t/
batted	jogged	tossed

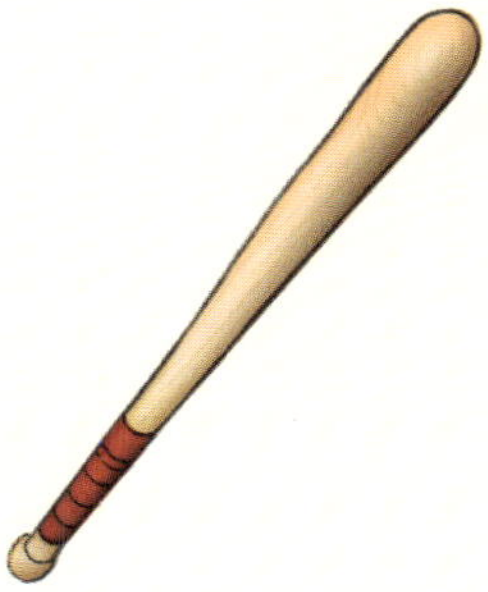

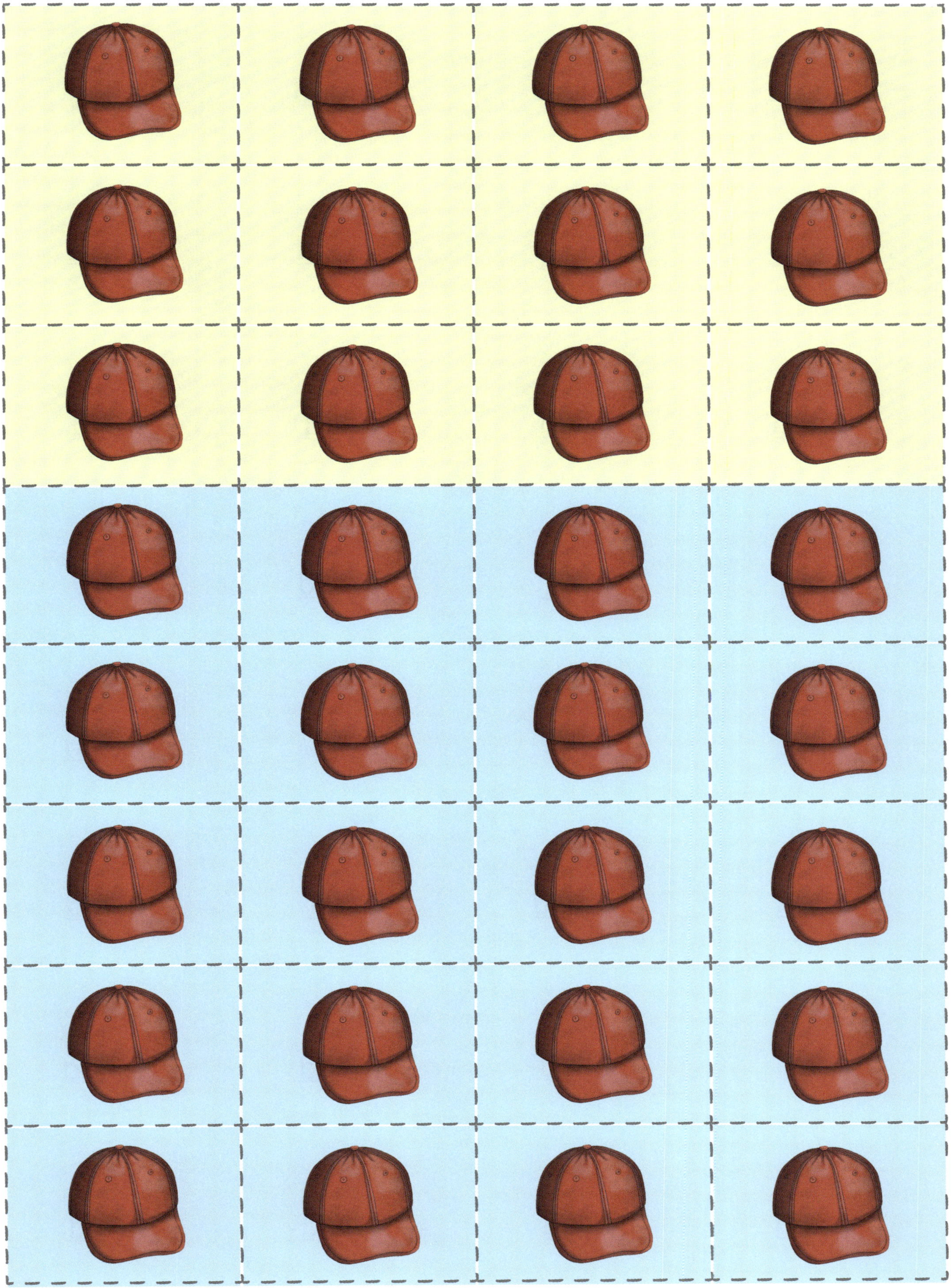

planted	yelled	dropped	waited
twisted	fixed	thanked	landed
wanted	asked	missed	ended
patted	stayed	stepped	rained
needed	boiled	mixed	snowed
started	cleaned	locked	spoiled
folded	mailed	bumped	crashed
painted	played	clapped	soaked

M

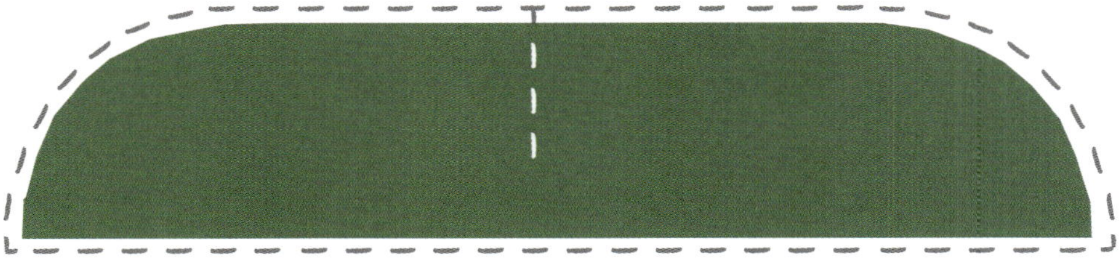

Writing Station

Words

1 ____________________

2 ____________________

3 ____________________

4 ____________________

5 ____________________

Sentences

1 ____

2 ____

3 ____

4 ____

5 ____

The Drop Silent E Rule

All About Spelling
Level 3, Lesson 22

Help the Bunnies

Let's help the bunnies add suffixes to base words that end in Silent E!

Is it a consonant suffix?	Is it a vowel suffix?
If so, just add the suffix to the base word.	If so, drop the Silent E before adding the suffix.

1. vote + ed = ____________
2. care + less = ____________
3. dance + ing = ____________
4. hope + ing = ____________

5. hike + er = ____________
6. hope + ful = ____________
7. save + ed = ____________

WHACK!
CRASH!
OUCH!

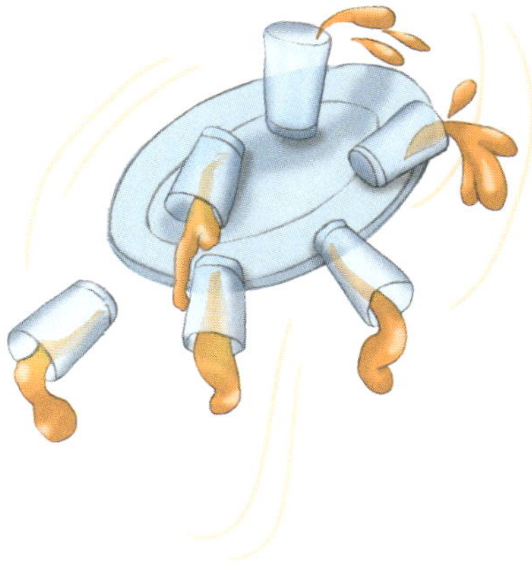

Writing Station

Words

1

2

3

4

5

Sentences

1

2

3

4

5

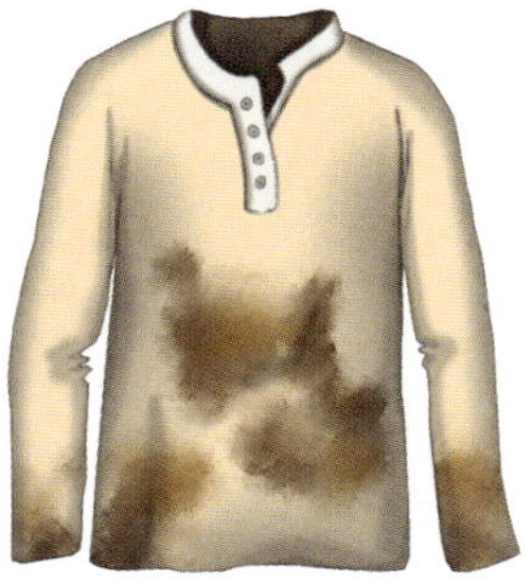

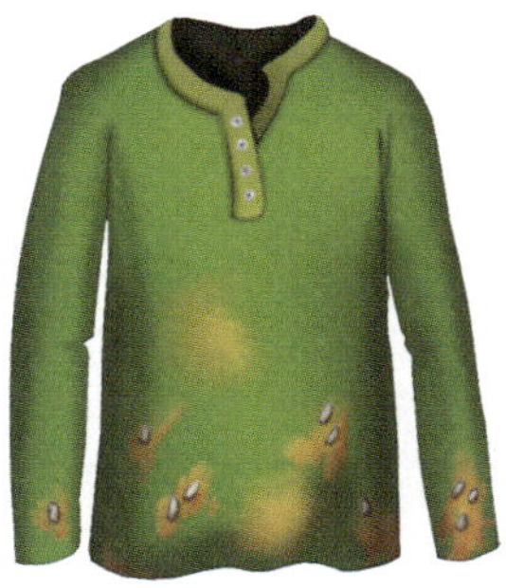

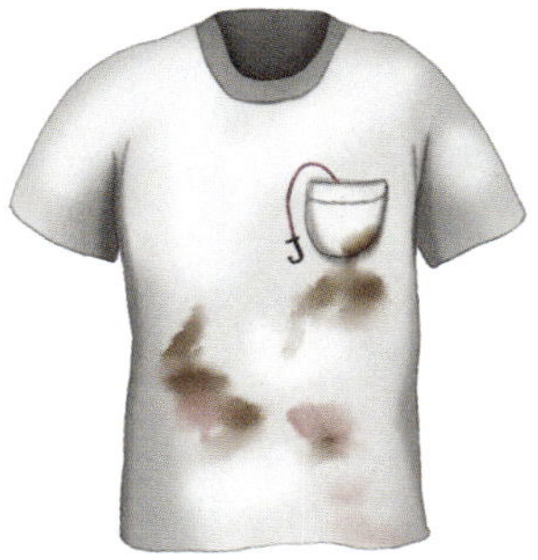

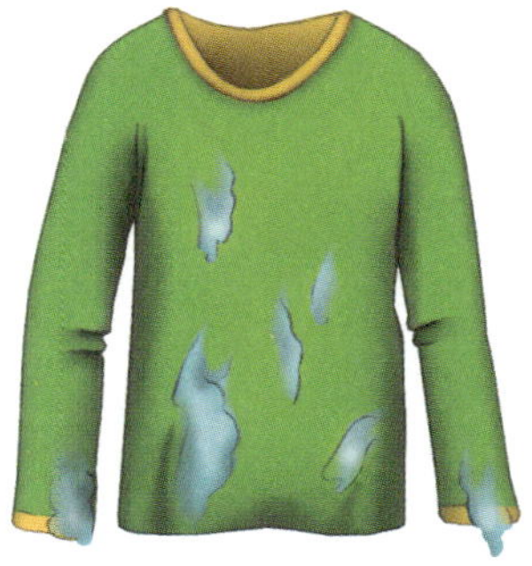

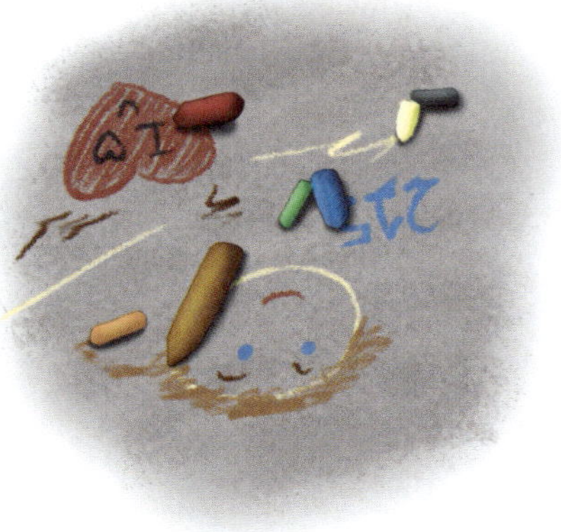

Word Bank for IR

swirl	firm	thirsty	shirt	first
circus	whir	twirl	birthday	circle

birth	thirty	stir	girl	thirteen
dirty	sir	bird	third	dirt
whirl	skirt	birch		

Writing Station

Words

1. ____________________

2. ____________________

3. ____________________

4. ____________________

5. ____________________

Sentences

1. ____________________

2. ____________________

3. ____________________

4. ____________________

5. ____________________

Advanced Application

1. ______like
2. head______
3. en______
4. ______stone
5. con______
6. ______ed
7. a______
8. ______ing
9. sweat______
10. ______pool
11. ______ament
12. ______ers

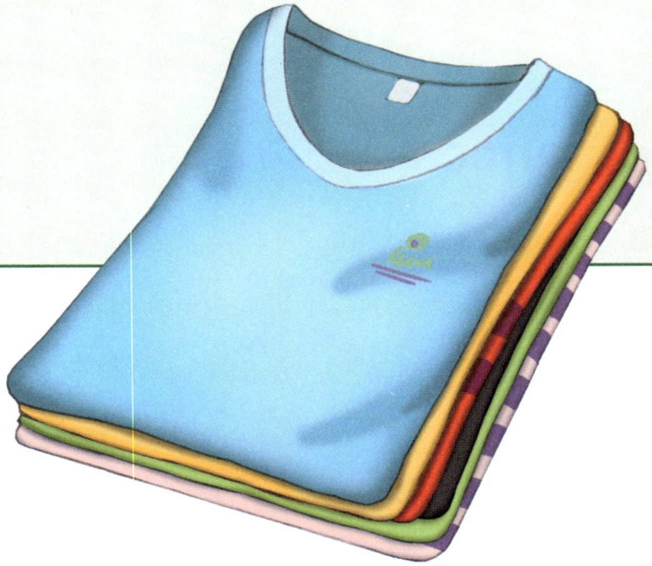

Word Sort for /er/

er	ur	ir
her	fur	bird

____________	____________	____________	____________
____________	____________	____________	____________
____________	____________	clerk	circle
silver	cracker	printer	fern
verb	term	insert	turtle
zipper	rubber	temper	spider
shelter	winter	over	iceberg
after	slurp	yogurt	birch

Writing Station

Words

1

2

3

4

5

Sentences

1

2

3

4

5

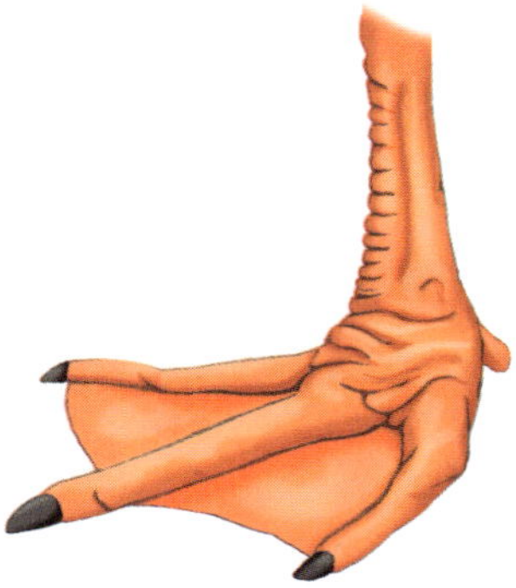

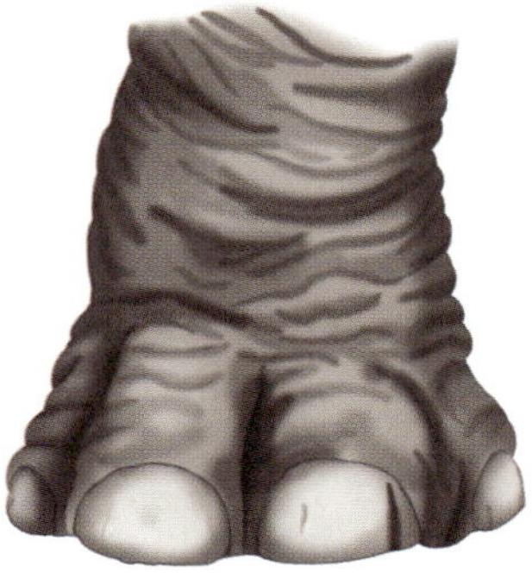

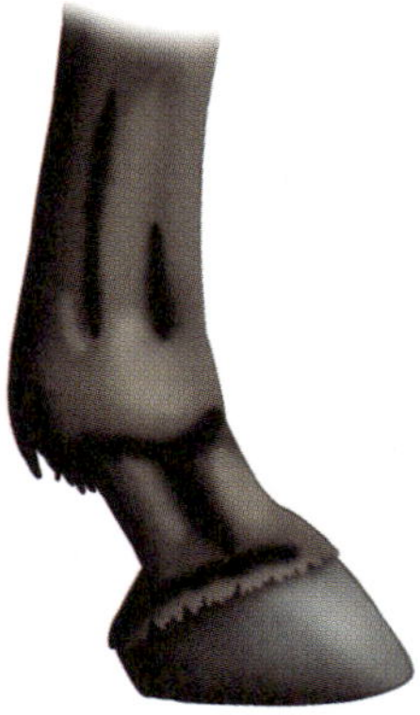

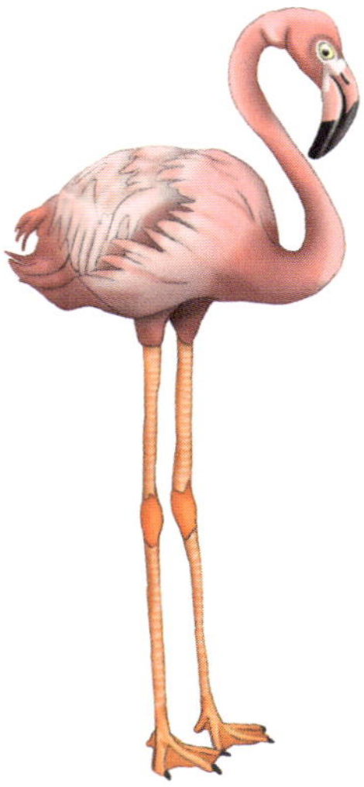

Writing Station

Words

1. ______________________

2. ______________________

3. ______________________

4. ______________________

5. ______________________

Sentences

1. ____

2. ____

3. ____

4. ____

5. ____

Advanced Application

1. ________ out
2. drift ________
3. ________ work
4. with ________
5. knight ________
6. ________ en
7. ________ byes
8. ________ falls
9. ________ worms
10. ________ alike
11. ________ beats
12. ________ edly

Tokay gecko

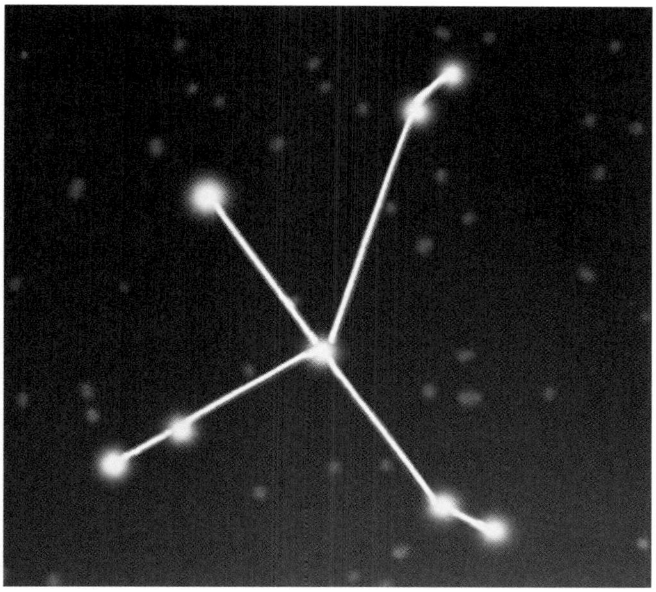

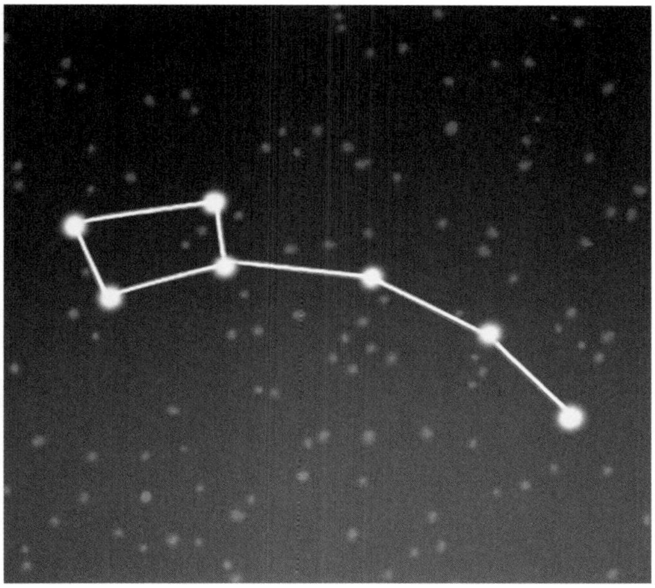

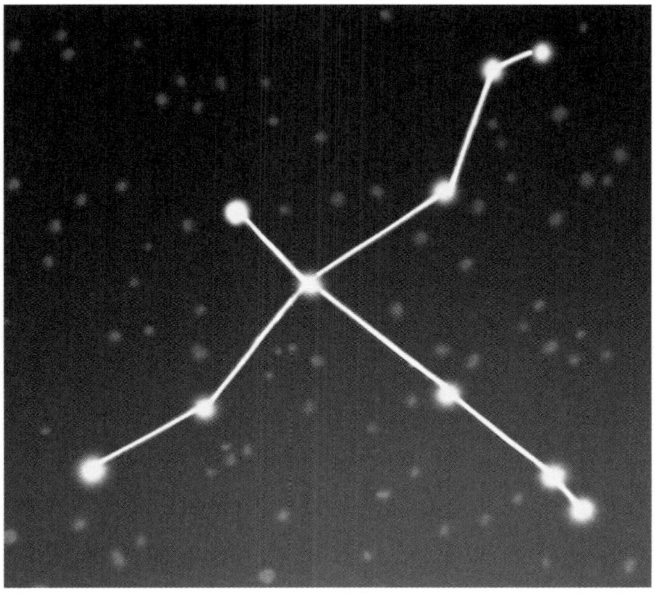

Aquila the Eagle

Big Dipper

Little Dipper

Canis Major

Cygnus the Swan

Orion

Writing Station

Words

1.
2.
3.
4.
5.

Sentences

1.
2.
3.
4.
5.

Advanced Application

1. ________rope
2. ________ing
3. fire________er
4. ________mare
5. ________seers
6. ________ening
7. ________ly
8. de________
9. up________
10. ________way
11. ________est
12. ________y

Word Sort for Long I

i	i-e	y	igh
find	mice	shy	night

____	____	____	____
____	____	____	____
____	____	kind	wild
blind	child	item	siren
tidy	ripen	advice	campfire
shine	bike	time	kite
life	bride	hive	vine
sky	by	fly	bright

Writing Station

Words

1

2

3

4

5

Sentences

1

2

3

4

5

The Change Y to I Rule

fry → fries
salty → saltiest
crispy → crispier
happy → happiness

If a word ends in single vowel Y, change the Y to I before adding a suffix.

All About® Spelling
Level 3, Lesson 28

Favorite Fries

penny

clay

sleepy

silly

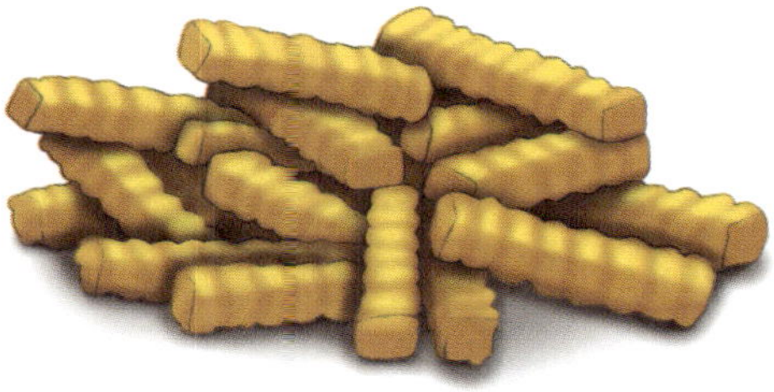

happy

easy

boy

Dip Your Fries

Let's add suffixes to words that end in Y!

Is it a single Y?	Is there a vowel before the Y?
Change the y to i before adding the suffix.	**Add the suffix without changing the base word.**

1. fry + ed = ____________
2. try + es = ____________
3. play + er = ____________
4. windy + er = ____________

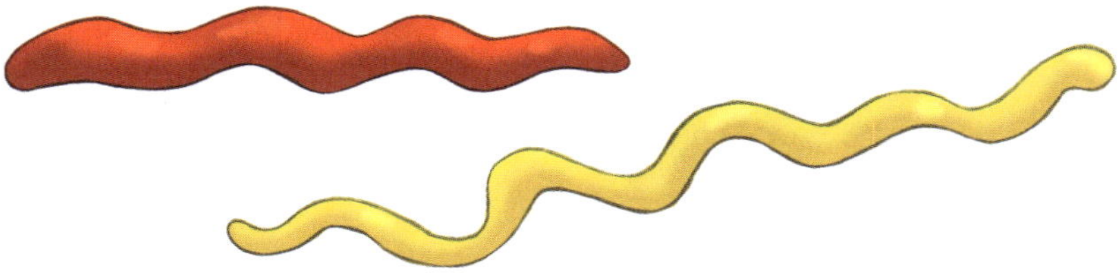

5. joy + ful = ____________
6. dry + ed = ____________
7. tray + s = ____________

Mustard
Gravy
Guacamole
Ranch
Ketchup
Cheese
BBQ Sauce
Chocolate Shake

FRENCH
Fries

Writing Station

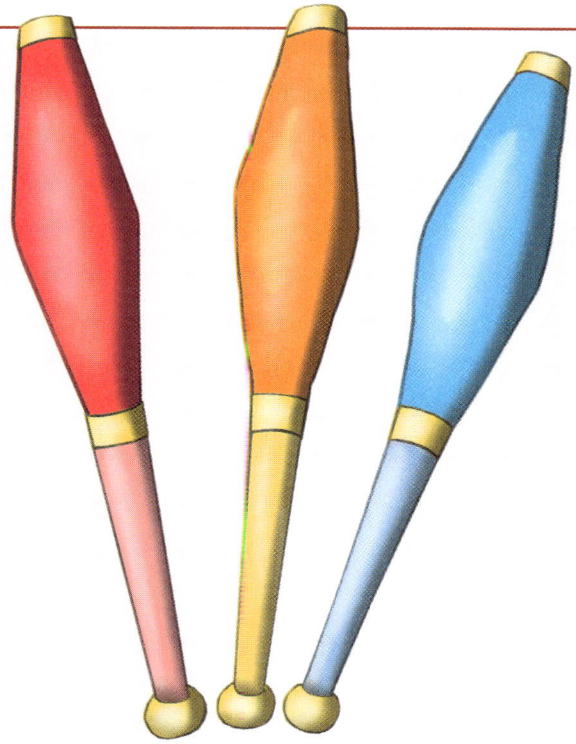

Words

1 ______________________

2 ______________________

3 ______________________

4 ______________________

5 ______________________

Sentences

1 ______________________

2 ______________________

3 ______________________

4 ______________________

5 ______________________

did not

she will

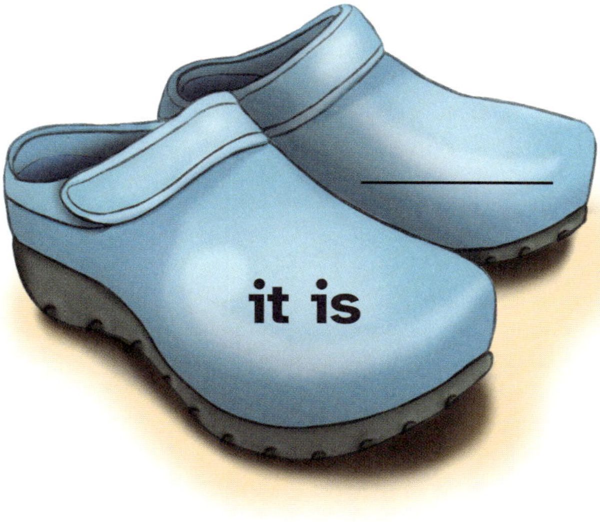
it is

are not

have not

you will

she'll

didn't

aren't

it's

you'll

haven't

I will

I am

can not

will not

what is

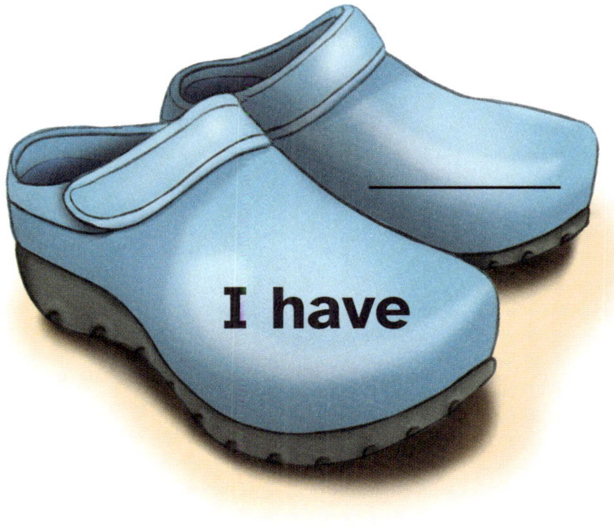
I have

I'm

I'll

won't

can't

I've

what's

My Lost Shoes

Hey, can you help me? ______ getting ready to go play and I ______ find my shoes! ______ looked in all the usual places, and I ______ know where they are!

______ so frustrating! Mom ______ seen them. Dad says ______ my job to find my own shoes because ______ busy looking for his phone and his glasses. ______ sure ______ find his things soon, and I hope I ______ have to look too long for mine!

My shoes ______ on the porch, and I ______ seen them under the bed. I ______ see them in the closet, but ______ hard to tell with all the books and clothes ______ crammed in there. I ______ look in the attic because I ______ want to go up there. ______ dusty and dark and ______ what spiders like. No thanks!

______ have to excuse me. If I ______ find my shoes soon, ______ have to stay indoors forever! Oh, wait— ______ that on my feet?

My shoes! I found them! Right where I left them, too. Thanks for helping me look! ______ the best!

My Lost Shoes

Hey, can you help me? I'm getting ready to go play and I can't find my shoes! I've looked in all the usual places, and I don't know where they are!

It's so frustrating! Mom hasn't seen them. Dad says it's my job to find my own shoes because he's busy looking for his phone and his glasses. I'm sure he'll find his things soon, and I hope I don't have to look too long for mine!

My shoes aren't on the porch, and I haven't seen them under the bed. I didn't see them in the closet, but it's hard to tell with all the books and clothes I've crammed in there. I didn't look in the attic because I don't want to go up there. It's dusty and dark and that's what spiders like. No thanks!

You'll have to excuse me. If I don't find my shoes soon, I'll have to stay indoors forever! Oh, wait—what's that on my feet?

My shoes! I found them! Right where I left them, too. Thanks for helping me look! You're the best!

Writing Station

Words

1 ____________

2 ____________

3 ____________

4 ____________

5 ____________

Sentences

1 ____________

2 ____________

3 ____________

4 ____________

5 ____________

Jelly

1 It makes me want to

2 What it is made of

3 Best spread on

4 What you use to eat it

5 How it tastes

Here Are 6 Great Reasons to Have a Pony

1. 

____ never have to guess who ____ your last ____ ____ .

2. 

____ off your pony and landing in a ____ ____ will make you ____ .

3. 

Watching a ____ ____ kick a ____ to the ____ is ____ .

4.  You'll have the ____ memories, like the ____ the squirrel ____ the gate and all the ____ got ____ .

5.  You won't mind ____ up ____ floors! There will ____ a time when your ____ kicks over a ____ bucket with its ____ and you will think it's cute.

6.  While your ____ may help you achieve your ____ of ____ in a horse show, it may also ____ ____ over the neighbor's fence!

What NOT to Do When Camping

1.

_______ store _______ in your tent unless you like sharing with _______ raccoons.

2.

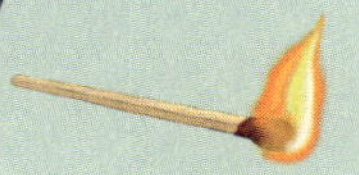

Don't forget your matches unless you like _______ potatoes and cold _______ .

3.

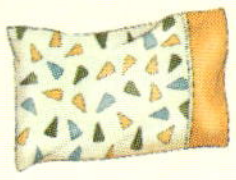

Don't pitch your tent in a _______ spot or _______ end up with a _______ _______ .

4.

Don't forget your ______ in case you have to go to the ______ in the ______ of the ______.

5.

Don't forget other ______ camping essentials like swim trunks, a ______ box, and ______ ______.

6.

And finally, ______ don't laugh at the ______ sleeping on logs in the sun. It ______ their feelings.

Certificate of Achievement

All About® Spelling

awarded to

____

for successfully completing Level 3

______________________________ Teacher's Signature

__________ Date